Inspector General
United States
Department *of* Defense

Evaluation of DoD Accident Reporting

MEMORANDUM FOR UNDER SECRETARY OF DEFENSE FOR ACQUISITION,
        TECHNOLOGY, AND LOGISTICS
        ASSISTANT SECRETARY OF DEFENSE FOR HEALTH AFFAIRS
        DEPUTY ASSISTANT SECRETARY OF THE ARMY FOR
            ENVIRONMENT, SAFETY, AND OCCUPATIONAL HEALTH
        DEPUTY ASSISTANT SECRETARY OF THE NAVY FOR
            SAFETY
        DEPUTY ASSISTANT SECRETARY OF THE AIR FORCE FOR
            ENVIRONMENT, SAFETY, AND OCCUPATIONAL HEALTH

SUBJECT: Evaluation of DoD Accident Reporting (Report No. SPO-2010-007)

     We are providing this report for information and use. We requested and received comments from the staffs of the Under Secretary of Defense for Acquisition, Technology, and Logistics; the Assistant Secretary of Defense for Health Affairs; and the responsible Deputy Assistant Secretaries of the Army, the Navy, and the Air Force.

     All the offices concurred with the relevant recommendations in this final report. Management also provided technical comments that we considered in the preparation of this final report.

     We appreciate the courtesies extended to the staff. Please direct questions to Mr. George Marquardt at (703) 604-9159 (DSN 664-9159) or Dr. Sardar Hassan at (703) 604-9146 (DSN 664-9146).

                                 Kenneth P. Moorefield
                                 Deputy Inspector General
                                 for Special Plans and Operations

Results in Brief: Evaluation of DoD Accident Reporting

What We Did

The DoD Military Injury Prevention Priorities Working Group analyzed a sample of the 1,874,826 injuries recorded in the CY 2004 medical databases. The Working Group reported a large disparity between military medical records for accident-related injuries and Service safety center records for accidents. At the request of the Assistant Deputy Under Secretary of Defense for Environment, Safety, and Occupational Health, we evaluated the DoD injury reporting process for reportable injury-causing accidents involving civilian and military personnel. We also reviewed DoD and Component policies, reporting requirements, and recording systems for injury-causing accidents.

What We Found

Although a significant part of the large discrepancy between medical databases and safety databases could be attributed to the differences in recording criteria, non-compliance also contributed. Installation and unit safety offices rarely reported accidents below the "Class C" level. Database discrepancies for in-patient cases were an indication that Component safety offices also may not have captured reports for all Class C and higher accidents. Quantifying the extent of non-compliance would require further analysis of medical database entries and was outside the scope of this evaluation.

DoD and Service policies did not incorporate requirements included in memoranda previously issued by the Under Secretary of Defense for Acquisition, Technology, and Logistics. Further, the Assistant Secretary of Defense for Health Affairs had not issued policy concerning the sharing of accident-related medical data with DoD safety offices. As a result, information sharing between safety and medical organizations, concerning injury-causing accidents, was ineffective.

What We Recommend

This report presents 13 recommendations. The key recommendations are summarized below:

The Under Secretary of Defense for Acquisition, Technology, and Logistics should revise DoD Instruction 6055.07 to incorporate changes required by earlier memoranda; eliminate confusion between "reportable" and "recordable" as related to accidents; and direct Component safety offices to obtain accident information from medical organizations, worker's compensation programs, and other relevant sources to supplement information reported directly by injured personnel. The Under Secretary of Defense for Acquisition, Technology, and Logistics should also initiate a review of DoD Component execution of injury record keeping requirements by directly comparing the current number of injuries recorded in DoD Component mishap records to the estimated number of mishap-related injuries recorded in military medical treatment records.

The Assistant Secretary of Defense for Health Affairs should clarify Health Insurance Portability and Accountability Act provisions, and direct DoD medical commands to collect accident information during injury treatment and provide relevant data to DoD safety offices.

DoD Components should develop procedures for using worker's compensation notifications to supplement accident reporting to safety offices, and establish medical liaison at their respective safety centers to coordinate activities and programs with Service medical communities.

Client Comments

The Office of the Under Secretary of Defense for Acquisition, Technology, and Logistics and the Office of the Assistant Secretary of Defense for Health Affairs concurred with the applicable recommendations included in this final report. Please refer to Appendix E for related information on revisions to the draft recommendations.

The Offices of the responsible Deputy Assistant Secretaries of the Army, the Navy, and the Air Force concurred with the applicable recommendations in the draft report.

Recommendations Table

Client	Recommendations Requiring Comment	No Additional Comments Required
Under Secretary of Defense for Acquisition, Technology, and Logistics		1.a, 1.b, 1.c, 1.d, 3
Assistant Secretary of Defense for Health Affairs		2.a, 2.b
Deputy Assistant Secretary of the Army for Environment, Safety, and Occupational Health		4, 7, 8, 9
Deputy Assistant Secretary of the Navy for Safety		5, 7, 8
Deputy Assistant Secretary of the Air Force for Environment, Safety, and Occupational Health		6, 8

Total Recommendations in this Report: 13

Table of Contents

Introduction

Preventable accidents in DoD result in an average of over 800 deaths per year[1] and degrade capabilities and readiness. Accidents also generate significant costs. Since 2001, average annual cost of workers' compensation claims for the civilian workforce was over $600 million. Accident-related costs for military personnel are not easily identified, but in a December 2001 report,[2] the National Safety Council estimated annual military workplace compensation cost to be approximately $3.2 billion. The Council further estimated overall direct and indirect costs (schedule delays, training and retraining of replacement workers, increased insurance premiums, and added administrative fees) related to preventable accidents to be $12 to $20 billion per year. In addition, the report stated that preventable accidents lower the morale of personnel and result in poorer customer relations.

DoD Safety professionals rely on accurate information to reduce preventable accidents and associated costs. This report reviews DoD reporting systems to identify problem areas that prohibit effective reporting of injuries resulting from accidents.

Background

DoD Directive 4715.1E, "Environment, Safety, and Occupational Health," March 19, 2005, promulgated by the Under Secretary of Defense for Acquisition, Technology, and Logistics [USD(AT&L)] is the overarching policy for the safety, environment, and occupational health programs. The Directive assigns safety program responsibilities to DoD senior officials including the Under Secretary of Defense for Personnel and Readiness [USD(P&R)]:

- USD(AT&L) – provide oversight of safety programs, to include: measuring, auditing, and reporting on performance; validating resource requirements; designating the DoD Designated Agency Safety and Health Official; resolving management disputes between or among DoD Components; maintaining an awards program; and supporting the Defense Safety Oversight Council.
- USD(P&R) – establish objectives, guidance, and procedures across all USD(P&R) organizations to manage safety risks, identify asset requirements, and measure and report performance; participate in asset performance reviews; and chair the Defense Safety Oversight Council.

DoD Instruction 6055.7 "Accident Investigation, Reporting, and Record Keeping," October 3, 2000, prescribes and enforces regulations directly related to investigation, reporting, and keeping records on accidental death, injury, occupational illness, and property damage. On December 3, 2004, the USD(AT&L) issued a memorandum (Appendix B) changing DoD Instruction 6055.7 to comply with the updated Occupational Safety and Health Administration occupational injury

---

[1] Defense Manpower Data Center data "U.S. Active Duty Military Deaths – 1980 through 2006," obtained from http://siadapp.dmdc.osd.mil/personnel/CASUALTY/Death_Rates.pdf, accessed on March 23, 2010. See Appendix A for further discussion.

[2] Department of Defense Executive Assessment of Safety and Occupational Health Management Systems, National Safety Council, December 6, 2001, Appendix E (pg.78-80).

and illness recording and reporting requirements contained in Code of Federal Regulations, Title 29, Part 1960, Subpart 1.[3]

On July 19, 2005, USD(P&R), in his capacity as the Chair of the Defense Safety Oversight Council, tasked the Assistant Secretary of Defense for Health Affairs [ASD(HA)] to "identify the top 5 causes of non-combat injuries and recommend mitigation initiatives to reduce injuries." To facilitate that effort, on September 1, 2005, the ASD(HA) formed the DoD Military Injury Prevention Priorities (DMIPP) Working Group. Participants included representatives from environment, health, and safety communities in OSD, major DoD Components, and Joint Staff. The goal of the DMIPP Working Group was to outline a systematic, coordinated DoD approach to injury prevention.

In February 2006, the DMIPP Working Group published a report analyzing injury data for calendar year 2004.[4] The report summarized 1,874,826 accident-related injuries of all types: 1,858,200 ambulatory / outpatient cases, 16,137 injuries requiring hospitalization, and 489 fatalities.

In its analysis, the DMIPP Working Group reported a significant disparity between military medical records reflecting the number of accident-related injuries and Service safety center records of accidents (See Figure 1). The DMIPP Working Group attempted to match medical to safety records for the top five types of injuries. The Working Group found that of the 2,273 in-patient cases in medical record databases, only 539 (24 percent) were present in the Service safety center records. For ambulatory / outpatient cases, the matching was 2 percent – of total 152,568 medical entries, only 3,016 cases were identified in the safety databases.

	TOTAL	Army	Navy	Air Force
In-patient cases	24.0%	14.5%	22.7%	52.7%
	(539 of 2,273)	(184 of 1270)	(132 of 580)	(223 of 423)
Out-patient cases	2.0%	0.6%	1.5%	4.2%
	(3,016 of 152,568)	(387 of 60,945)	(698 of 45,553)	(1,931 of 46,070)

Figure 1. DMIPP Working Group reported Service Safety-Medical Data Matching Results

The DMIPP Working Group report prompted action from the Office of the USD(AT&L). On February 20, 2007, the USD(AT&L) issued a memorandum (Appendix C) replacing the memorandum of December 3, 2004. USD(AT&L) directed the Heads of DoD Components to:

- Establish procedures for the collection, maintenance, analysis, and reporting of injuries and illnesses

---

[3] Code of Federal Regulations, Title 29, "Labor," Chapter XVII, "Occupational Safety And Health Administration, Department Of Labor," Part 1960, "Basic Program Elements For Federal Employee Occupational Safety And Health Programs And Related Matters," 2004. Most recent update in 2009.
[4] http://oai.dtic.mil/oai/oai?verb=getRecord&metadataPrefix=html&identifier=ADA458257

- Include the use of military medical treatment information and civilian personnel injury information to identify reportable accidents
- Maintain records of accident investigation reports involving all DoD civilian employees "pursuant to Code of Federal Regulations, Title 29, Part 1904"[5]
- Apply civilian personnel reporting procedures to "separate, but equivalent logs" for military personnel injuries and illnesses

In addition, personnel were required to notify their supervisors of all work-related accidents, injuries, and illnesses as soon as possible.

On April 24, 2008, the Office of the USD(AT&L) issued Change 1 to DoD Instruction 6055.7 that renumbered the Instruction from 6055.7 to 6055.07, updated references, and added requirements for mishap analysis and resolution of friendly fire incidents. However, Change 1 did not incorporate the modifications contained in the February 20, 2007, memorandum.

Objective

The objective of this project was to evaluate the DoD injury reporting process for reportable accidents involving civilian and military injuries. Specifically, we focused on:

- identifying DoD injury reporting policies
- evaluating compliance with reporting requirements
- identifying root causes for under-reporting to safety centers
- determining impediments to data transfer between medical and safety systems
- determining the impact of incompatibility of data among DoD Components

For this project, the term "injury," refers to an injury caused by a reportable accident. Also, the terms "Accident Reporting" and "Accident / Injury Reporting" refer to reportable accidents as listed in DoD Instruction 6055.7, "Accident Investigation, Reporting, and Record Keeping," October 3, 2000, as modified by USD(AT&L) Memorandum, "Injury Reporting Requirements," February 20, 2007.

Scope and Methodology

We reviewed DoD and Component policies, general compliance with policy, and data systems regarding reporting of injuries resulting from accidents. We reviewed DoD and military Service policies and procedures for reporting accidents resulting in injuries. We also reviewed data systems at the Service Safety Centers, Office of the Secretary of Defense, and the DoD Civilian Personnel Management Service (CPMS) regarding injuries to military and civilian personnel. We concentrated on DoD and military Service processes. Installation visits provided examples of system application. Our review excluded accidents that did not result in injuries and all accidents in areas of ongoing contingency operations.

---

[5] Code of Federal Regulations, Title 29, "Labor," Chapter XVII, "Occupational Safety And Health Administration, Department Of Labor," Part 1904, "Recording And Reporting Occupational Injuries And Illnesses."

We discussed the status of data transfer from the medical databases to safety databases and injury data management practice with responsible officials from the:

- Office of the Assistant Secretary of Defense for Health Affairs
- U.S. Army Center for Health Promotion & Preventive Medicine
- Armed Forces Health Surveillance Center (a DoD Executive Agency supported by U.S. Army Center for Health Promotion & Preventive Medicine)
- Office of the Deputy Under Secretary of Defense for Readiness
- Office of the Deputy Under Secretary of Defense for Business Transformation
- Office of the Deputy Assistant Secretary of Defense for Environment, Safety, and Occupational Health

We interviewed safety personnel in the Offices of the responsible Deputy Assistant Secretaries of the Army, the Navy, and the Air Force. We visited the Army Combat Readiness and Safety Center, the Naval Safety Center, and the Air Force Safety Center to obtain a detailed picture of the accident reporting process and medical / safety cooperation in each Department.

We made site visits to one installation from each military department. In addition to interviewing the personnel at each installation safety office and installation medical facility visited, we interviewed personnel from three or more operational units. For each operational unit, we interviewed at least three enlisted personnel, one supervisor, and the unit safety officer. Our interview sample at the installations was not sufficient to allow for generalized conclusions regarding Department-wide implementation and compliance. General conclusions in this report are based on data from Department safety offices and safety centers.

Comments concerning the occupational accident and injury reporting process for civilian personnel were derived from interviews with the Chief of the Injury and Unemployment Compensation Division of the CPMS. We also interviewed safety officials at the Defense Logistics Agency and Fort Bragg, North Carolina. At Fort Bragg we also met supervisors of units with large numbers of civilian employees.

The Army Audit Agency conducted an audit of the Army accident reporting process concurrent with this review. We coordinated our site visits with the Army Audit Agency to avoid duplication of effort and to reduce impact on the Army installation and safety offices. Cooperation provided us the opportunity to interview safety personnel at the Army National Guard Headquarters, Army Medical Command, and Army Materiel Command.

Use of Computer-Processed Data

For this project we used summary data provided by DoD organizations and offices including the DMIPP Working Group, Defense Manpower Data Center, and military Department Safety Centers / Safety Offices. We did not verify the reliability of the data provided. While we used the summary data to support our observations, the data sets were not material to our conclusions.

Observations

Observation 1 – Policies and Practices Regarding Collection and Use of Military Medical Treatment Data

Condition

The degree of information sharing between safety and medical organizations for injury-causing accidents varied among the three military departments. Safety organizations throughout DoD were not actively pursuing accident information available from the medical databases. Medical organizations were not providing data to safety professionals. There was no agreement in the safety community about the distinction between the terms "reportable accidents" and "recordable accidents."

Cause

We identified the following potential causes for the above condition.

(a) Office of the Under Secretary of Defense for Acquisition, Technology, and Logistics did not:
- incorporate all relevant changes mandated by the various preceding memoranda issued since October 3, 2000.
- clarify the requirement to "collect and use" military medical treatment information (as opposed to just "use").
- address the confusion created by two very similar terms, "reportable accidents" and "recordable accidents."

(b) Safety training provided by the Components did not sufficiently emphasize reporting of all accidents (regardless of duty status and impact) to supervisors.

(c) The Assistant Secretary of Defense for Health Affairs did not:

- issue policy to DoD Components clarifying the fact that the Health Insurance Portability and Accountability Act allows sharing of injury-related medical data with the DoD safety offices.
- issue any memorandum directing the DoD Component medical organizations to collect accident information during injury treatment and provide the data to corresponding DoD safety offices.

Effects

Mishap-related injury data, available in the military medical databases, were not being fully utilized by the Component Safety offices to identify unreported mishaps. Therefore, Component Safety Centers had incomplete accident databases. Also, Service members were not aware of the safety policy requirements for reporting all accidents.

Recommendations

Recommendation 1:

The Under Secretary of Defense for Acquisition, Technology, and Logistics should revise DoD Instruction 6055.07, "Accident Investigation, Reporting, and Record Keeping: Change 1 of April 24, 2008" to:

    a. Incorporate all relevant changes required by the Under Secretary of Defense for Acquisition, Technology, and Logistics memoranda issued since October 3, 2000.

    b. Eliminate confusion between the terms "reportable accidents" and "recordable accidents," as well as between "accident reporting" and "accident recording."

    c. Clarify the requirement to "collect and use" military medical treatment information (as opposed to just "use") to aid in mishap identification.

    d. Require DoD Components to provide safety training emphasizing reporting of accidents to supervisors regardless of duty status and impact.

Recommendation 2:

The Assistant Secretary of Defense for Health Affairs should:

    a. Issue policy to DoD Components clarifying that Health Insurance Portability and Accountability Act allows sharing of injury-related medical data with DoD safety offices.

    b. Direct DoD Component medical organizations to collect accident information during injury treatment and provide the information to corresponding DoD safety offices.

Detailed Discussion & Analysis

Accident Reporting Mechanisms

Figure 2 below illustrates the two-mechanism reporting process for military personnel. The event sequence for the traditional or primary mechanism is shown in the top row. The back-up or secondary mechanism, which is available to capture data not reported through the traditional mechanism, is shown in the bottom row. USD(AT&L) memorandum of February 20, 2007, required safety offices to access and utilize this secondary mechanism. The illustration also highlights the steps where accident records can be lost.

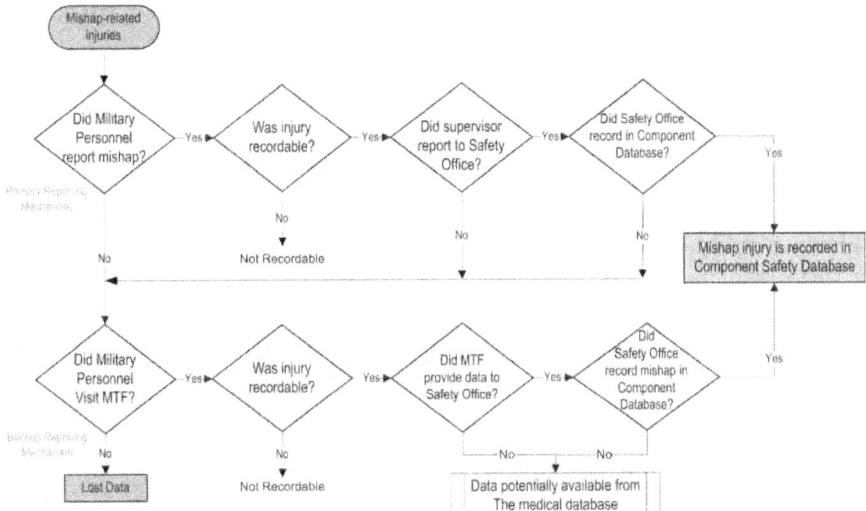

Figure 2. Military Personnel Accident-Related Injury Reporting Process

Safety Community

Office of the Secretary of Defense

The USD(AT&L) memorandum of February 20, 2007, directed the Heads of DoD Components to use "military medical treatment information and civilian personnel injury information in order to identify [reportable] accidents." However, the Office of the USD(AT&L) did not incorporate that requirement into the subsequent Change 1 of DoD Instruction 6055.07, issued on April 24, 2008. Component safety offices did not develop comprehensive procedures to obtain relevant military medical treatment information from treatment facilities or other medical sources. Safety offices were limited to military medical treatment information provided to them directly by injured personnel. Existing DoD policy was insufficient to cause appropriate Component action.

Military Departments

Service members, interviewed at the three installations we visited, were not aware of the safety policy requirements for reporting all accidents. During the interviews and in written responses, military personnel at installations stated that they report accidents and occupational injuries to their immediate supervisor only if they miss any work. Some supervisors whom we interviewed demonstrated limited knowledge of safety policies and were not aware of the purpose of reporting minor accidents: identification of cumulative impact, analysis of trends, and development of preventive steps. Supervisors and unit safety officers were not trained to request information about unreported accidents from Service members.

Representatives of the Office of the USD(AT&L) explained that the intent of the memorandum of February 20, 2007, was for medical information to supplement existing accident reporting and contribute to safety risk assessments. None of the military departments were meeting the full intent of revised DoD Instruction 6055.07 included in the USD(AT&L) memorandum of February 20, 2007. In fact, most installation safety personnel indicated that they were unaware of the USD(AT&L) memorandum of February 20, 2007. As of January 2010, the military departments had adopted different approaches to meet the requirement to use military medical treatment information.

Army

Army Regulation 385-10, "The Army Safety Program," August 23, 2007, did not require installation safety offices or unit safety offices to collect military medical information from medical treatment facilities or unit medical stations.

The Army safety office indicated that it was common practice for installation and/or unit safety offices to collect military injury information from installation medical treatment facilities. Our observations at the Fort Bragg medical facility and the installation safety office did not support this assertion. According to a brigade safety officer in the 82nd Airborne Division, his unit did not have any procedures to collect or to receive any accident data from the brigade medical office or installation medical treatment facility. In September 2007, the Army developed a data use agreement between the "Patient Administration Systems and Biostatistics Activity" and the "U.S. Army Combat Readiness / Safety Center." Service-wide accident related injury data now can be transferred to the Service safety center electronically. The Army Combat Readiness and Safety Center reported that as of March 2010, they received two data sets from the Patient Administration Systems and Biostatistics Activity. However, we did not receive any information concerning the use of these data or any plan for future data transfer.

Navy

As of January 2010, Navy safety policies (Navy Instruction 5102.1D and Marine Corps Order P5102.1D, "Mishap and Safety Investigation, Reporting, And Record Keeping Manual," January 7, 2005) did not require on-shore installation and unit safety offices to collect or receive military medical information from installation medical facilities.

During a site visit to Norfolk Naval Station, ship safety officers stated they had a good working relationship with ship medical officers and shared accident-related injury data. However, on-shore installation and unit safety officers had a lesser degree of cooperation and sharing with on-shore medical facilities.

Air Force

Air Force Instruction 91-204, "Safety Investigations and Reports," September 24, 2008, required installation-level safety offices to obtain accident information from installation medical facilities. Medical community at the Andrews AFB also had procedures for collecting accident information from patients in the emergency room and providing the information to the installation safety office.

Air Force policies and procedures came closest to meeting the requirements of the February 20, 2007, USD(AT&L) memorandum. However, we saw no arrangement for the transfer of accident information from in-hospital stays or clinic visits. Air Force Safety Center personnel indicated that all installations were supposed to have the same procedures. However, they had not verified that all installations had developed a similar process for emergency room visits.

Service Safety Centers

Personnel at the Service Safety Centers indicated that they were aware of the February 20, 2007, USD(AT&L) memorandum. However, it appears that they did not understand the changes directed by the memorandum. They believed that the memorandum contents were a repetition of the December 2004 USD(AT&L) memorandum, which required them to revise policies to comply with the Occupational Safety and Health Administration's reporting requirements contained in Code of Federal Regulations, Title 29, Part 1904.

Medical Community

The ASD(HA) is the principal advisor to the USD(P&R) for all DoD health policies, programs, and force health protection activities. As of January 2010, ASD(HA) had not issued policy concerning the sharing of accident-related medical injury data with DoD safety offices at bases and installations.

DoD 6025.18-R, "Health Information Privacy Regulation," January 24, 2003, prescribes the uses and disclosures of protected health information. While it allows disclosure of health information for workers' compensation and the release of data to several entities with varying degrees of sanitization, the policy contains no explicit statement concerning sharing of data with DoD safety offices at the installation level. This contributed to differing interpretations of privacy law and hindered systematic sharing of accident-related data with safety offices.

We observed that the Andrews Air Force Base medical group was sharing information from the medical treatment facility emergency room with the installation safety office. This cooperation was the result of policy published by the Air Force Air Mobility Command. The Air Force-specific program was generated prior to the requirement in the USD(AT&L) memorandum of February 20, 2007.

We found no similar program within the Army or the Navy. Army and Navy installation safety officers indicated that their medical counterparts were reluctant to share information and cited concerns about potential violation of Health Insurance Portability and Accountability Act provisions. Representatives from the Army and the Navy installation medical facilities stated that the Office of the ASD(HA) had not made data sharing between medical and safety a requirement. Medical organization representatives also stated that they were unaware of the need to share military medical treatment information with the safety community. This demonstrates a failure to effectively communicate among functional areas and the military Services.

Observation 2 – Analysis of Accident Reporting

Condition

As of the date of this report, the DoD does not have an accurate measure of the degree of non-compliance in accident reporting. Although the DMIPP Working Group report indicated a high degree of discrepancy between the medical databases and the Service safety databases, it also indicated that underreporting (non-compliance in reporting) is not the only cause for the discrepancy. Other factors include differences in threshold reporting requirements and poor data quality.

Cause

The DMIPP Working Group compared all injuries in the medical databases to the entries in the Service safety databases for matching, including injuries from: action of a hostile force, intentionally self-damaging acts, attack or assault, pre-existing musculoskeletal disorders, minimum stress and strain, escaping or eluding custody or arrest, and the illegal use of drugs or other substances. However, these injuries are not reportable as per DoD Instruction 6055.07. In addition, medical databases include injuries that are below Class C and occur during off-duty hours. DoD Instruction 6055.07 of February 20, 2007, did not provide clear directions regarding accidents below Class C. As shown in Appendix D, Army and Air Force safety policy developed definitions for Class D accidents. Injuries included in Class D are less severe than the injuries included in Class C, but more severe than injuries requiring first aid only.

Effects

DoD and the Components are unable to evaluate their performance in the area of accident reporting. The impacts of policy changes on completeness of accident reporting cannot be verified.

Recommendation

> ### *Recommendation 3:*
>
> The Under Secretary of Defense for Acquisition, Technology, and Logistics should initiate a review of DoD Component execution of injury record keeping requirements by directly comparing the current number of injuries recorded in DoD Component mishap records to the estimated number of mishap-related injuries recorded in military medical treatment records.

Observation 3 – Other Military Personnel Issues

All Military Departments

Officials from the Office of the USD(AT&L) requested that we determine if there was "any evidence that Service personnel are instructed to minimize reporting accidents that may make the unit look bad." We included a question in the questionnaire regarding this item. During interviews, we asked the questions to more than 30 Service members and included the query in a questionnaire. Personnel of various ranks indicated that the opposite was true – they were told by commanders to report all accidents. We found no indication of pressure from unit commanders to skip accident reporting.

Army

Condition

During our visit to Fort Bragg, the installation safety office informed us that the unit safety officers do not always notify the installation safety office when reporting accidents to the Army Combat Readiness / Safety Center through the Automated Reporting Accident System. Army Combat Readiness / Safety Center representatives later verified that this was an Army-wide issue, not unique to Fort Bragg. Many Army installation safety offices receive incomplete notifications about accidents on their installations.

Cause

In most cases, installation safety officers were part of the Army Installation Management Command, and not in the chain of command between units and the Combat Readiness / Safety Center. In addition, in the Automated Reporting Accident System for reporting Army mishaps, it was optional for the unit safety officers to notify the installation safety office.

Effects

Army installation safety officers had an incomplete picture of mishaps on their installations and they were unable to take all the necessary actions to prevent mishap recurrence.

Recommendation

> ***Recommendation 4:***
>
> The Deputy Assistant Secretary of the Army for Environment, Safety, and Occupational Health should modify the Automated Reporting Accident System to include automatic notification to the relevant installation safety office for on-base accidents at any Army installation.

Navy

Condition

Although Navy policy required ship and shore elements to use the Web Enabled Safety System for accident reporting, its implementation was inconsistent and incomplete.

Cause

Many commands and vessels reported mishaps and injuries using legacy reporting systems. Transfer of data between the systems was not automatic, creating the potential for data loss. In addition, shipboard personnel indicated that using the Web Enabled Safety System for accident reporting was difficult during deployment because of limited available bandwidth. A senior DoD official (former navy submarine officer) stated that it could also be a case of not assigning a high enough priority to accident reporting.

Effects

As a result of incomplete fielding of the accident reporting system, the Naval Safety Center was not receiving all of the accident reports. Also, many accident reports came in late.

Recommendation

> **_Recommendation 5:_**
>
> The Deputy Assistant Secretary of the Navy for Safety should expedite completion of fielding of the Web-Enabled Safety System throughout all commands and vessels, replacing the legacy reporting systems.

Air Force

Condition

At Andrews Air Force Base, we observed that while the installation and Major Command safety officers had access to the Air Force Safety Automated System, the unit safety officers had to manually complete accident reporting forms and fax them to their installation safety officer for entry into the automated system. The installation safety officer then manually entered the data into the Air Force Safety Automated System (after checking for reporting criteria). Discussions with Air Force Safety Center representatives confirmed that the procedure was Air Force-wide.

Cause

The Air Force is concerned about providing unit safety officers with access to the Air Force Safety Automated System because many of the unit safety officers are not full-time safety personnel.

Effects

The installation safety office is overwhelmed with the additional task of manually entering all of the accident reports into the Air Force Safety Automated System. There is a lag between the time when the unit safety officer reports the mishap and when the data appear in the Air Force Safety Automated System. The existing process is inefficient.

Recommendation

> ### *Recommendation 6:*
>
> The Deputy Assistant Secretary of the Air Force for Environment, Safety, and Occupational Health should modify the Air Force Safety Automated System to allow unit safety offices to enter accident reports into the system.

Service Safety Centers

Condition

The Army Combat Readiness and Safety Center and Naval Safety Center did not have a dedicated medical liaison to coordinate policy development and implementation with the medical community.

Cause

The Army and the Navy were unaware of the need for a designated medical liaison at their safety centers. The Navy was also limited by budgetary constraints.

Effects

The Army and the Navy did not receive routine accident data from their military medical facilities, while the Air Force has been receiving a daily set of accident records from the emergency rooms.

Recommendation

> ### *Recommendation 7:*
>
> The Deputy Assistant Secretary of the Army for Environment, Safety, and Occupational Health and the Deputy Assistant Secretary of the Navy for Safety should establish medical liaisons at their respective safety centers to coordinate activities and programs with Service medical communities.

Observation 4 – Civilian Personnel Issues

Military Departments

Condition

According to DoD Civilian Personnel Management Service (CPMS), approximately 12 percent of the 22,000 Safety First Event Reporting notifications sent each year did not reach the intended recipient – designated points of contact in the unit safety offices.

Figure 3 below shows the two-mechanism accident reporting process required for DoD civilians. The back-up mechanism (shown in the bottom row of the flowchart), as required by USD(AT&L) memorandum of February 20, 2007, utilizes Safety First Event Reporting notifications to identify missed accident reports.

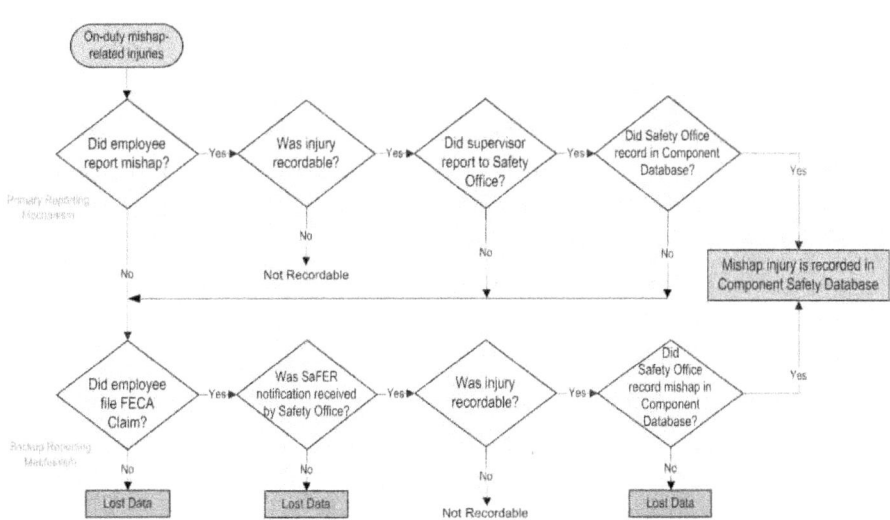

Figure 3. Civilian Personnel Accident-Related Injury Reporting Process

Cause

According to CPMS, the primary cause was invalid e-mail addresses resulting from personnel turn over at the safety offices. In addition, the Navy and the Air Force did not set up comprehensive procedures for the use of Safety First Event Reporting notifications. Moreover, not all Army installation safety offices used this reporting system.

Effects

As a result of non-receipt of notifications by the unit safety offices, at least 2,600 accident reports did not enter the back-up mechanism for data capture. This increased the potential for additional data loss but, more importantly, presented incomplete visibility to concerned organizations and leaders.

Recommendation

> **_Recommendation 8:_**
>
> The Deputy Assistant Secretary of the Army for Environment, Safety, and Occupational Health; Deputy Assistant Secretary of the Navy for Safety; and Deputy Assistant Secretary of the Air Force for Environment, Safety, and Occupational Health should develop common procedures for using Safety First Event Reporting notifications to enhance completeness of DoD accident reporting. This should include maintaining accurate contact information for the installation and unit safety offices at the Civilian Personnel Management Service.

Army Reporting System for Injuries involving Civilians

Condition

We observed that at Fort Bragg, the installation safety office used the Army Safety Performance Improvement and Reporting system, a legacy system not connected to the Army Combat Readiness and Safety Center. The Army Safety Office representative identified three Army installations still using the Army Safety Performance Improvement and Reporting system, although Army policy required the use of the Automated Reporting Accident System. In December 2009, the Fort Bragg safety office notified us that Fort Bragg had discontinued the use of the Army Safety Performance Improvement and Reporting system.

Cause

As per the Army Safety Office, three Army installations were using the legacy system (Army Safety Performance Improvement and Reporting system) because their safety offices were unaware of the mandatory requirement to use the Automated Reporting Accident System for civilian personnel.

Effects

Accident databases at the Army Combat Readiness / Safety Center were missing accident reports for civilian personnel from these three Army installations and understating the incidence of accidents.

Recommendation

> **_Recommendation 9:_**
>
> The Deputy Assistant Secretary of the Army for Environment, Safety, and Occupational Health should direct all Army installations to ensure that installation safety offices are using the Army Automated Reporting Accident System for reporting all injuries - including injuries involving civilians.

Appendix A. Active Duty Military Fatalities

The Defense Manpower Data Center provided a summary of all U.S. active duty military deaths from 1980 through 2007. The table below shows that over the 28-year period, a total of 23,558 deaths were caused by accidents, representing over half of the total deaths from all causes. Perhaps of even greater significance, from 2002 to 2007, a period of combat operations, active duty fatalities from preventable accidents (3,476) were as high as fatalities from all hostile actions (3,451).

U.S. ACTIVE DUTY MILITARY DEATHS - 1980 through 2007 (as of April 22, 2008)							
Calendar Year	Total Military FTE*	Total Deaths	Deaths by Hostile Action	Deaths Caused by Accidents	Cause Assignment Pending	Accident-related Deaths per 100K FTE	Accident Deaths as % of Total Deaths
1980	2,159,630	2,392	1	1,556		72	65.1%
1981	2,206,751	2,380		1,524		69	64.0%
1982	2,251,067	2,319	2	1,493		66	64.4%
1983	2,273,364	2,465	281	1,413		62	57.3%
1984	2,297,922	1,999	7	1,293		56	64.7%
1985	2,323,185	2,252	5	1,476		64	65.5%
1986	2,359,855	1,984	2	1,199		51	60.4%
1987	2,352,697	1,983	39	1,172		50	59.1%
1988	2,309,495	1,819	17	1,080		47	59.4%
1989	2,303,384	1,639	23	1,000		43	61.0%
1990	2,258,324	1,507	1	880		39	58.4%
1991	2,198,189	1,787	147	931		42	52.1%
1992	1,953,337	1,293	1	676		35	52.3%
1993	1,849,537	1,213	29	632		34	52.1%
1994	1,746,482	1,075		544		31	50.6%
1995	1,661,928	1,040	7	538		32	51.7%
1996	1,613,675	974	20	527		33	54.1%
1997	1,578,382	817		433		27	53.0%
1998	1,538,570	827	3	445		29	53.8%
1999	1,525,942	796		439		29	55.2%
2000	1,530,430	758	17	397		26	52.4%
2001	1,552,096	891	58	434		28	48.7%
2002	1,627,142	999	18	543		33	54.4%
2003	1,732,632	1,410	340	576	1	33	40.9%
2004	1,711,916	1,873	739	605	3	35	32.3%
2005	1,664,014	1,941	739	649	5	39	33.4%
2006	1,611,533	1,882	769	559	25	35	29.7%
2007	1,608,226	1,950	846	544	70	34	27.9%
Total	53,799,705	44,265	4,111	23,558	104	44	53.2%
Per Year	1,921,418	1,581	171	841		44	53.2%

* Official Department of Defense end-strengths as of December 31 for military pay accounts. Excludes full time Guard and Reserve. Full time equivalent (FTE) is based on official Department of Defense fiscal year end selected reserve strength (10% of the figure is used to estimate days on Active Duty).

Prepared by the Data, Analysis, and Programs Division of the Defense Manpower Data Center.

Appendix B. USD(AT&L) Memorandum – "Safety and Health Recordkeeping"

THE UNDER SECRETARY OF DEFENSE
3010 DEFENSE PENTAGON
WASHINGTON, D.C. 20301-3010

ACQUISITION,
TECHNOLOGY
AND LOGISTICS

DEC 3 2004

MEMORANDUM FOR SECRETARIES OF THE MILITARY DEPARTMENTS
CHAIRMAN OF THE JOINT CHIEFS OF STAFF
UNDER SECRETARIES OF DEFENSE
ASSISTANT SECRETARIES OF DEFENSE
ASSISTANTS TO THE SECRETARY OF DEFENSE
DIRECTOR OF ADMINISTRATION AND MANAGEMENT
DIRECTOR, PROGRAM ANALYSIS AND EVALUATION

SUBJECT: Safety and Health Recordkeeping

This memorandum clarifies procedures in DoDI 6055.7, Accident Investigation, Reporting and Recordkeeping, pertaining to recordkeeping requirements.

The Occupational Safety and Health Administration (OSHA) is developing a final rule amending the occupational injury and illness recording and reporting requirements applicable to Federal agencies (29 CFR Part 1960, Subpart I), including the forms used by Federal agencies to record those injuries and illnesses. The final rule will make the Federal sector's recordkeeping and reporting requirements essentially identical to the private sector. Recordkeeping under the revised rule is a prerequisite to enrollment in the Voluntary Protection Program. Therefore, paragraph E.4.8.6 of DoDI 6055.7, Accident Investigation, Reporting and Recordkeeping, October 3, 2000 is deleted and paragraph E.4.8.1 is replaced with:

E4.8.1. Safety and Health Recordkeeping. Records shall be maintained for civilian personnel at each DoD installation or distinctly separate DoD activity using the attached guidance detailing changes in 29 CFR part 1960. Separate accounting for on- and off-duty accidents will be maintained for military personnel.

This memorandum is effective immediately. DoD Instruction 6055.7 governing Accident Investigation, Reporting and Recordkeeping shall be updated in 180 days. We will field web-based tools to aid in implementation and data consolidation.

Michael W. Wynne
Acting

Attachment:
As stated

Department of Defense
Revised Safety and Health Recordkeeping Requirements

Subpart A—General

3. 29 CFR part 1960, Subpart A, is revised to read as follows:

§ 1960.2 Definitions.

* * * * *

(l) Injury or Illness. An injury or illness is an abnormal condition or disorder. Injuries include cases such as, but not limited to, a cut, fracture, sprain, or amputation. Illness includes both acute and chronic illnesses, such as, but not limited to, a skin disease, respiratory disorder, or poisoning.

* * * * *

Subpart D—Inspection and Abatement

4. 29 CFR part 1960, subpart D, is revised to read as follows:

§1960.29 Accident Investigation

* * * * *

(b) In any case, each accident which results in a fatality or the hospitalization of three or more employees shall be investigated to determine the causal factors involved. Except to the extent necessary to protect employees and the public, evidence at the scene of an accident shall be left untouched until inspectors have an opportunity to examine it.

* * * * *

Subpart I—Recordkeeping and Reporting Requirements

5. 29 CFR part 1960, Subpart I, is revised to read as follows:

§1960.66 Purpose, scope and general provisions.

I

(a) The purpose of this Subpart is to establish uniform requirements for collecting and compiling by agencies of occupational safety and health data, for proper evaluation and necessary corrective action, and to assist the Secretary in meeting the requirement to develop and maintain an effective program of collection, compilation, and analysis of occupational safety and health statistics.

(b) Except as modified by this Subpart, Federal agency injury and illness recording and reporting requirements shall comply with the requirements under 29 CFR 1904, Subparts C, D, E, and G, except that the definition of "establishment" found in 29 CFR 1960.2(h) will remain applicable to Federal agencies."

(c) Each agency shall utilize the information collected through its management information system to identify unsafe and unhealthful working conditions, and to establish program priorities.

(d) The provisions of this subpart are not intended to discourage agencies from utilizing recordkeeping and reporting forms which contain a more detailed breakdown of information than the form provided by the Department of Labor. Because of the unique nature of the national recordkeeping program, Federal agencies must have recording and reporting requirements that are the same as Part 1904 for determining which injuries and illnesses will be entered into the records and how they are entered. All other injury and illness recording and reporting requirements used by any Federal agency may be more stringent than, or supplemental to, the requirements of Part 1904, but must not interfere with the agency's ability to provide the injury and illness information required by Part 1904.

(e) Information concerning occupational injuries and illnesses or accidents which, pursuant to statute or Executive Order, must be kept secret in the interest of national defense or

2

foreign policy shall be recorded on separate forms. Such records shall not be submitted to the Department of Labor but may be used by the appropriate Federal agency in evaluating the agency's program to reduce occupational injuries, illnesses and accidents.

Note to § 1960.66: The recording or reporting of a work-related injury, illness or fatality does not mean that the Federal agency or employee was at fault, that an OSHA rule has been violated, or that the employee is eligible for workers' compensation or other benefits. The requirements of this Part do not diminish or modify in any way a Federal agency's responsibilities to report or record injuries and illnesses as required by the Office of Workers' Compensation Programs under the Federal Employees' Compensation Act (FECA), 5 USC 8101 et seq.

§1960.67 Federal Agency Certification of the Injury and Illness Annual Summary (OSHA 300-A or equivalent)

As required by 29 CFR 1904.32, a company executive must certify that he or she has examined the OSHA 300 Log and that he or she believes, based on his or her knowledge of the process by which the information was recorded, that the annual summary is correct and complete. For Federal establishments, the person who performs the certification shall be one of the following: (1) the senior establishment management official, (2) the head of the Agency for which the senior establishment management official works, or (3) any management official who is in the direct chain of command between the senior establishment management official and the head of the Agency.

Note to §1960.67: This modification to the requirement for certification of Federal agency injury and illness records is necessary because the private sector position titles contained in the regulation do not fit the Federal agency position titles for agency executives. The federal

3

officials listed in this paragraph are intended to be the equivalent of the private sector officials who are required to certify records under 1904.32(b)(4).

§1960.68 Prohibition against discrimination.

Title 29 CFR 1904.36 refers to Section 11 (c) of the Occupational Safety and Health Act. For Federal agencies, the words "Section 11(c)" shall be read as "Executive Order 12196 Section 1-201(f)."

Note to §1960.68: This modification is necessary because Section 11(c) of the Occupational Safety and Health Act only applies to private sector employers and the U.S. Postal Service. The corresponding prohibitions against discrimination applicable to Federal employers are contained in Section 1-201(f) of Executive Order 12196.

§1960.69 Transition from former rule and retention and updating of old forms.

(a) Between October 1, 2004 and January 1, 2005, agencies must continue to record and track their occupational injuries and illnesses. During that period, Federal agencies may choose to comply with the requirements of the old Part 1960, Subpart I, or they may choose to comply with the requirements of 29 CFR 1904.

(b) Federal agencies must retain copies of the recordkeeping records utilized under the old system for five years following the year to which they relate and continue to provide access to the data as though these forms were the OSHA Form 300 Log and Form 301 Incident Report. Agencies are not required to update the old forms.

§1960.70 Reporting of serious accidents.

Agencies must provide the Office of Federal Agency Programs with a summary report of each fatal and catastrophic accident investigation. The summaries shall address the date/time of accident, agency/establishment named and location, and consequences, description of operation

4

and the accident, causal factors, applicable standards and their effectiveness, and agency corrective/preventive actions.

Note to §1960.70: This paragraph is retained from the previous regulation 29 CFR 1960.70 paragraph (e). The requirements of this paragraph are in addition to the requirements for reporting fatalities and multiple hospitalization incidents to OSHA under 29 CFR 1904. 39.

§1960.71 Agency annual reports.

(a) The Act and E.O. 12196 require all Federal agency heads to submit to the Secretary an annual report on their agency's occupational safety and health program, containing such information as the Secretary prescribes.

(1) Each agency must submit to the Secretary by January 1 of each year a report describing the agency's occupational safety and health program of the previous fiscal year and objectives for the current fiscal year. The report shall include a summary of the agency's self-evaluation findings as required by 1960.78(b).

(2) The Secretary must provide the agencies with the guidelines and format for the reports at the time they are requested.

(3) The agency reports will be used in preparing the Secretary's report to the President.

(b) The Secretary will submit to the President by October 1 of each year a summary report of the status of the occupational safety and health of Federal employees based on agency reports, evaluations of individual agency progress and problems in correcting unsafe or unhealthful working conditions, and recommendations for improving their performance.

5

Appendix C. USD(AT&L) Memorandum – "Injury Reporting Requirements"

THE UNDER SECRETARY OF DEFENSE
3010 DEFENSE PENTAGON
WASHINGTON, DC 20301-3010

ACQUISITION,
TECHNOLOGY
AND LOGISTICS

FEB 2 0 2007

MEMORANDUM FOR SECRETARIES OF THE MILITARY DEPARTMENTS
CHAIRMAN OF THE JOINT CHIEFS OF STAFF
UNDER SECRETARIES OF DEFENSE
DIRECTOR, DEFENSE RESEARCH AND ENGINEERING
ASSISTANT SECRETARIES OF DEFENSE
GENERAL COUNSEL OF THE DEPARTMENT OF DEFENSE
INSPECTOR GENERAL OF THE DEPARTMENT OF DEFENSE
DIRECTOR, OPERATIONAL TEST AND EVALUATION
ASSISTANTS TO THE SECRETARY OF DEFENSE
DIRECTOR OF ADMINISTRATION AND MANAGEMENT
DIRECTOR, FORCE TRANSFORMATION
DIRECTOR, NET ASSESSMENT
DIRECTORS OF DEFENSE AGENCIES
DIRECTORS OF THE DOD FIELD ACTIVITIES

SUBJECT: Injury Reporting Requirements

The following policy direction revises injury reporting requirements of DoDI 6055.7, "Accident Investigation, Reporting and Recordkeeping," and replaces policy memo "Safety and Health Recordkeeping," December 3, 2004.

A recent review showed significant underreporting of military injuries resulting in lost duty time. Failure to report and investigate mishaps prevents us from acquiring the knowledge needed to prevent future injuries.

The attached guidance, which is effective immediately, requires injured military and civilian personnel and their supervisors to report each mishap-related injury. It also requires the use of medical treatment and civilian workers compensation reports in the identification of mishaps. The next issuance of DoD Instruction 6055.7 shall incorporate this guidance.

Kenneth J. Krieg

Attachment:
As stated

Injury Reporting Requirements

Change to DoDI 6055.7, "Accident Investigation, Reporting and Recordkeeping"

Responsibilities

The Heads of the DoD Components shall:

- Establish procedures to ensure the collection, maintenance, analysis, and reporting of standardized property damage, injury, and occupational illness data for Class A, B, and C accidents and for OSHA recordable injuries and illnesses. The procedures shall include the use of military medical treatment information and civilian personnel injury information in order to identify accidents to be reported. Reporting procedures shall not interfere with either the timely reporting of accidents or the settling and payment of claims arising from property damage, injury, and occupational illness.
- Pursuant to 29 CFR 1904, maintain records of accident investigation reports for all Class A, B, and C accidents involving DoD civilian employees, including a log of injuries and illnesses for all DoD installations and distinctly separate DoD activities within an installation or across multiple installations.
- Concerning military personnel, apply civilian personnel reporting procedures and definitions in maintaining and annotating separate but equivalent logs for injuries and illnesses.
- Insure that all reporting and record-keeping protects the privacy interests of DoD military and civilian personnel and complies with DoD 5400.11-R, Department of Defense Privacy Program.

Supervisors and managers shall:

- Complete DoD Component notification requirements to their supervisory chain of command, within one working day of receiving information relative to an accident, injury or, illness, and
- Assist with accident investigations.

Non-supervisory Personnel shall:

- Notify the appropriate supervisor of all work-related accidents, injuries, and illnesses as soon as possible, but no later than the end of the shift or the day of occurrence. These mishaps include those related to duties performed while on Temporary Duty (TDY) status or, for civilian personnel, in any other location

1   Attachment

while in official duty status. For military personnel, these mishaps include injuries and occupational illnesses occurring on or off-duty.

Definitions

Class C Accident (revised from DoDI 6055.7). The resulting total cost of property damage is $20,000 or more, but less than $200,000; or a nonfatal injury or illness that results in one or more days away from work, not including the day of the injury.

Days Away From Work. Days on which a person looses time from work as a result of an injury or illness, starting with the day after the injury occurred or the illness began, and including calendar days the person was unable to work, regardless of whether or not the person was scheduled to work on those days (see 29 CFR § 1904.7(b)(3)). For military personnel, days away from work for on- and off-duty injuries and occupational illnesses include hospitalizations, medical restrictions to quarters, convalescent leave, and commander directed removal from duties.

Days of Restricted Work or Transfer to Another Job. Days on which a person is working, but restricted from completing assigned tasks or transferred to another task to accommodate the injury or illness (see 29 CFR § 1904.7(b)(4)). Calendar days not scheduled to work are included in the count of days. Count of days is stopped when the person is either returned to their pre-injury/illness job or permanently assigned to a job that has been modified or permanently changed to eliminate the routine functions the person was restricted from performing. For military personnel, restricted work or transfer to another job includes limited and light duty assignments.

First Aid (revised from DoDI 6055.7). Minor treatment for injury or illness as defined in 29 CFR 1904.7(b)(5)(ii), regardless of the professional status of the person providing the treatment.

Recordable Injury and Illness. For civilian personnel, an occupational injury or illness meeting the recording requirements of 29 CFR § 1904.7(a) including: death, days away from work, restricted work or transfer to another job, medical treatment beyond first aid, loss of consciousness, or a significant injury or illness diagnosed by a physician or other licensed health care professional. For military personnel, an on-duty injury or occupational illness meeting the recording requirements of 29 CFR § 1904.7(a) including: death, days away from work, job transfer or restriction of work activity, medical treatment beyond first aid, loss of consciousness, or a significant on--duty injury or occupational illness diagnosed by a physician or other licensed health care professional; or an off-duty injury resulting in death or one or more days away from work.

Appendix D. Military Department Definitions for Accidents below Class C Threshold

The military Departments developed procedures for reporting Class C and higher category accidents through central databases located at their Safety Centers. Army and Air Force safety policies developed definitions for accidents below the Class C threshold, calling them "Class D" accidents. We found that safety professionals generally consider Class D accidents as less severe than Class C, but more severe than injuries requiring first aid only.

Army Regulation 385-10, "The Army Safety Program," August 23, 2007, establishes Army policy and defines Class D accidents as "an Army accident in which the resulting total cost of property damage is $2,000 or more, but less than $20,000; a nonfatal injury or illness resulting in restricted work, transfer to another job, medical treatment greater than first aid, needle stick injuries and cuts from sharps that are contaminated from another person's blood or other potentially infectious material, medical removal under medical surveillance requirements of an OSHA standard, occupational hearing loss, or a work–related tuberculosis case."

OPNAVINST 5102.1D, "Navy & Marine Corps Mishap and Safety Investigation, Reporting, And Record Keeping Manual," of January 7, 2005, establishes Navy and U.S. Marine Corps safety policy but does not define accidents below the Class C threshold.

Air Force Instruction 91-204, "Safety Investigations and Reports," September 24, 2008, establishes Air Force policy and defines Class D accidents as "Any nonfatal injury or occupational illness that does not meet the definition of Lost Time. These are cases where, because of injury or occupational illness, the employee only works partial days, has restricted duties or was transferred to another job, required medical treatment greater than first aid, or experienced loss of consciousness (does not include GLOC) [G-force induced loss of consciousness]. In addition, a significant injury (e.g. fractured/cracked bone, punctured eardrum) or occupational illness (e.g. occupational cancer (mesothelioma), chronic irreversible disease (beryllium disease)) diagnosed by a physician or other licensed health care professional must be reported even if it does not result in death, days away from work, restricted work, job transfer, medical treatment greater than first aid, or loss of consciousness."

Appendix E. Client Comments

Office of the Under Secretary of Defense for Acquisition, Technology, and Logistics

The response from the Office of the USD(AT&L) to our draft report follows (see pages 33 to 35). Management non-concurred with four recommendations in the draft report: 1.c, 1.d, 3.a, and 3.b. We discussed the concerns with management officials and we agreed to:

- Revise recommendation 1.c
- Delete recommendation 1.d and renumber original 1.e as 1.d
- Revise recommendations 3.a and 3.b and combine them into a single recommendation (#3)

This final report includes revised language, and the Office of the USD(AT&L) concurred with the revised recommendations.

Office of the Assistant Secretary of Defense for Health Affairs

The response from the Office of the ASD(HA) to our draft report follows (see pages 36 to 39). Management non-concurred with two recommendations - 3.a and 3.b. After discussions and negotiations with applicable offices, we revised the recommendations 3.a and 3.b into a single recommendation (#3) directed only at the Office of the USD(AT&L). The Office of the ASD(HA) is not responsible for implementing this revised recommendation #3. Management's non-concurrence is no longer an issue.

Military Department Offices of Primary Responsibility

The Offices of the Deputy Assistant Secretary of the Army for Environment, Safety, and Occupational Health; the Deputy Assistant Secretary of the Navy for Safety; and the Deputy Assistant Secretary of the Air Force for Environment, Safety, and Occupational Health concurred with the original recommendations. Their comments are available on request.

OFFICE OF THE UNDER SECRETARY OF DEFENSE
3000 DEFENSE PENTAGON
WASHINGTON, DC 20301-3000

ACQUISITION,
TECHNOLOGY
AND LOGISTICS

JUL 2 7 2010

MEMORANDUM FOR DEPUTY INSPECTOR GENERAL FOR SPECAIL PLANS
AND OPERATIONS

THROUGH: DIRECTOR, ACQUISITION RESOURCES AND ANALYSIS 7/28/10

SUBJECT: Response to DoDIG Draft Report, Evaluation of DoD Accident Reporting,
Project No. D2008-DIP0E2-0012.000

As requested, I am providing responses to the general content and
recommendations contained in the subject report.

Recommendation 1.a.:
Incorporate all relevant changes required by Under Secretary of Defense for
Acquisition, Technology, and Logistics Memorandums issued since October 3, 2000.

Response:
Concur. The draft revision to DoDI 6055.07 has incorporated the associated Directive
Type Memorandums. The draft revision with changes was distributed for coordination
on July 2, 2010. Completion of this recommendation will depend on successful
coordination.

Recommendation 1.b.:
Eliminate confusion between the terms "reportable accidents" and "recordable
accidents," as well as between "accident reporting" and "accident recording."

Response:
Concur. The draft revision to DoDI 6055.07 emphasizes requirements for
"recordkeeping" and "notification," and uses the term "reportable" only where useful
to the DoD Components. The draft revision was distributed for coordination on
July 2, 2010. Completion of this recommendation will depend on successful
coordination.

Recommendation 1.c.:
Strengthen the requirement to use "military medical treatment information" to meet
the intent of identifying missing accident-related information.

Response:

Non-Concur. We recognize the current shortcomings in DoD Component use of military medical treatment information to identify missing accident-related injury information. However, we believe the current policy provides sufficiently clear direction to the DoD Components. USD(AT&L) memo, "Injury Reporting Requirements," February 20, 2007, requires:

> "The Heads of the DoD Components shall:
> Establish procedures to ensure the collection, maintenance, analysis, and reporting of standardized property damage, injury, and occupational illness data for Class A, B, and C accidents and for OSHA recordable injuries and illnesses. The procedures shall include the use of military medical treatment information and civilian personnel injury information in order to identify accidents to be reported. ..."

The completeness of Component safety databases will improve when the Components implement existing DoD policy.

Recommendation 1.d.:

Require DoD Components to identify unreported accident-related injuries using all potential sources beyond direct reporting by the injured personnel.

Response:

Non-Concur. Current DoD policy requires Components to use military medical treatment information and civilian personnel injury information in order to improve the completeness of Component safety databases. Component actions to implement existing policy will improve the completeness of our safety databases. Other potential sources have not been identified and cannot be evaluated.

Recommendation 1.e.:

Require DoD Components to provide safety training emphasizing reporting of accidents to supervisors regardless of duty status and impact.

Response:

Concur. This recommendation was completed August 19, 1998, with issuance of DoDI 6055.1, "DoD Safety and Occupational Health Program."

> "E3.3.1.2. Supervisors. Train supervisors in the management skills needed to implement the DoD Component's SOH policies and programs. These skills include: ... accident reporting and investigation; ..."

Recommendation 3.a.:

Identify and quantify reportable, accident-related injuries captured by medical databases but not entered into safety databases.

Response:

Non-Concur. The comparison of injuries from medical databases to injuries in Military Service mishap databases was completed and published in the report, "DoD Military Injury Prevention Priorities Working Group: Leading Injuries, Causes and Mitigation Recommendations," 1 February 2006. This comparison was the initiator for the ADUSD(ESOH) request for this DoD IG assessment. Further comparison of injuries from medical databases to mishaps in safety databases provides no value until process improvements have been completed.

Recommendation 3.b.:

Establish procedures to monitor the impacts of policy changes on the completeness of Component safety databases.

Response:

Non-Concur. Procedures to monitor DoD Component program performance are currently established in DoDI 6055.1. However, federal agencies and private industry have not been able to develop adequate measures regarding the completeness of safety databases, leaving us with no satisfactory means of measure the impacts of policy changes on database completeness.

Our point of contact is ███████████████████████
████████████████

John Conger
Assistant Deputy Under Secretary of Defense
(Installations and Environment)

OFFICE OF THE ASSISTANT SECRETARY OF DEFENSE
WASHINGTON, DC 20301-1200

JUL 3 0 2010

HEALTH AFFAIRS

MEMORANDUM FOR DEPARTMENT OF DEFENSE INSPECTOR GENERAL
DEPUTY INSPECTOR GENERAL, SPECIAL PLANS AND
OPERATIONS

SUBJECT: Department of Defense Inspector General Draft Report, "Evaluation of DoD
Accident Reporting,"–Project No. D2008-DIPOE2-0012

As requested, we have provided responses to the recommendations provided by
the subject Report. We concur with most of the recommendations as written; however,
there are some recommendations that may have the Assistant Secretary of Defense
(Health Affairs) duplicating efforts or initiatives already performed or planned by the
Defense Safety Oversight Council and Under Secretary of Defense (Personnel and
Readiness) Defense Safety Enterprise System program. Although we may not disagree
with the intent of the recommendations, we proposed that another review of the scope of
these programs be made prior to making final recommendations that may lead to
duplication within the Department of Defense.

The point of contact on this audit is █████████████████████████████
███
███████████████████████

Charles L. Rice

Charles L. Rice, M.D.
President, Uniformed Services University of
the Health Sciences
Performing the Duties of the
Assistant Secretary of Defense
(Health Affairs)

Attachments:
As stated

**Department of Defense Inspector General DRAFT REPORT
D2008-DIPOE2-0012**

"Evaluation of DoD Accident Reporting"

RECOMMENDATION 2a: The Assistant Secretary of Defense for Health Affairs (ASD(HA)) should issue policy to Department of Defense (DoD) components clarifying Health Insurance Portability and Accountability Act (HIPAA) to allow sharing of injury-related medical data with DoD safety offices.

RESPONSE:

Concur. The Military Health System (MHS) implemented the Health and Human Services HIPAA Privacy Final Rule, by DoD 6025.18-R, Health Information Privacy Regulation, which permits limited sharing of injury-related medical data (see, e.g., DoD 6025.18-R, C7.2.1.1, C7.2.1.5, C7.11.1, C7.1). DoD 8580.02-R DoD Health Information Security Regulation, July 12, 2007, implements policy and assigns responsibilities for applying the standards for security of individually identifiable health information under parts 160, 162, and 164 of Title 45, Code of Federal Regulations. Based on your findings, clarifying HIPAA guidance for our MHS staff may be needed. However, the use and disclosure of the information by the safety offices falls under the Privacy Act of 1974.

RECOMMENDATION 2b: The ASD(HA) should direct DoD Component medical organizations to collect accident information during injury treatment and provide the data to corresponding DoD safety offices.

RESPONSE:

Concur. This recommendation follows the goal of not only DoD, but of the Nation, and efforts to institutionalize this documentation began in 2007. After a 3-year collaboration with the U.S. Army Center for Health Promotion and Preventive Medicine, the ICD-9-CM Coordination and Maintenance Committee, and the Center for Disease Control and Prevention's (CDC) National Center for Injury Prevention & Control, over 160 new external cause of injury codes were developed and accepted into the ICD 9 CM. The goal was to provide a national standard to better document information related to the injury at time of treatment to include status, mechanism, intent, location, and activity at time of injury. In October 2009, the final set added two new E-code sections - E000, External Cause Status, and E001–E030, Activity. Military Treatment Facilities are directed, through coding policies and electronic health record automation protocols, to use E-codes during injury treatment documentation. The permission to disclose this injury-related data for use by safety offices will be provided in the HIPAA clarification

Department of Defense Inspector General DRAFT REPORT
D2008-DIPOE2-0012

"Evaluation of DoD Accident Reporting"

guidance referenced above. My staff continues to work with CDC injury experts to develop strategies to improve national external cause-of-injury coding, which would improve our TRICARE providers.

RECOMMENDATION 3a: The Under Secretary of Defense for Acquisition, Technology, and Logistics (USD(AT&L)), in cooperation with the ASD(HA), should identify and quantify reportable, accident-related injuries captured by medical databases, but not entered into safety databases.

RESPONSE:

Non-concur. This recommendation seems to duplicate the mission of USD (Personnel and Readiness) (P&R) Defense Safety Enterprise System (DSES). MHS transfers all medical injury-related data on military personnel to the USD(P&R) DSES monthly. According to the Data Use Agreement with the TRICARE Privacy Office permitting the transfer of the health care data, "Data at the individual level will be merged with safety data at the involved personnel level. OSD can link medical information, e.g., length of hospital stay or ICD-9 codes, with specific safety incidents. This should provide a far more accurate picture of lost work days and their relationship to the actual mishaps. Differences in injury rates calculated from safety data are compared to those injury rates calculated from medical data. Using the merged data, associations related to injury events will be analyzed..." Thus, the DSES should be able identify and quantify the differences found in the safety data. I recommend a review of the mission and data use agreements of the DSES program before making this as a final recommendation.

RECOMMENDATION 3b: The USD(AT&L), in cooperation with the ASD(HA), establish procedures to monitor the impacts of policy changes on the completeness of Component safety databases.

RESPONSE:

Non-concur. This recommendation does not reflect the Defense Safety Oversight Council governance and scope of activities in this area. According to the Defense Safety Oversight Council (DSOC) Charter, 2006, the council shall:

2

**Department of Defense Inspector General DRAFT REPORT
D2008-DIPOE2-0012**

"Evaluation of DoD Accident Reporting"

"1. Review accident and incident trends, ongoing safety initiatives, private sector and other governmental agency best practices, and make recommendations to the Secretary of Defense for safety improvement policies, programs, and investments.

2. The Council will establish and monitor metrics to reduce DoD accidents and injuries by 75% of the Fiscal Year 2002 levels for each Military Department and the Defense Agencies by the end of FY 2008.

3. Assess, review and advise on improving all aspects of the coordination, relevance, efficiency, efficacy, timeliness and viability of existing DoD-wide safety and injury prevention information management systems."

The information provided by USD(P&R) DSES assists the DSOC and DoD in monitoring the impact of policy changes on safety databases.

I recommend review of the charter and programs of the DSOC before making this as a final recommendation.

NOTE: ADDITIONAL HEALTH-RELATED RESOURCES FOR SAFETY OFFICES

Currently, MHS provides de-identified medical information for safety and injury surveillance by way of the Armed Forces Health Surveillance Center (AFHSC). Each month, AFHSC uses the most currently available MHS data to provide a monthly summary of the number and types of injuries, by Service and installation, on its Web site. The data is de-identified and is intended to provide the health and safety offices a summary of what types of injuries are occurring on their installation and can be used to compare to what is being reported to their safety offices.

MHS providers have in place mechanisms to convey appropriate worker health information relative to their patient's condition to the command or supervisor. The command or supervisor may receive the following: duty restriction reports (profiles), convalescent leave documents, and quarters' information. This controlled transfer of information was developed to inform the commander/supervisor of the availability and limitations of a worker without compromising the patient's medical information. Commanders also are notified when their assigned personnel are hospitalized. It may be of concern to some commanders if safety offices receive information on their worker's medical status prior to notification through methods established in their policies.

3

Appendix F. Report Distribution

Office of the Secretary of Defense

Office of the Under Secretary of Defense for Acquisition, Technology, and Logistics*
Office of the Under Secretary of Defense for Personnel and Readiness
Office of the Assistant Secretary of Defense for Health Affairs*

Department of the Army

Inspector General, Department of the Army
Office of the Deputy Assistant Secretary for Environment, Safety, and Occupational
Health*

Department of the Navy

Naval Inspector General
  Deputy Naval Inspector General for Marine Corps Matters
Office of the Deputy Assistant Secretary for Safety*

Department of the Air Force

Inspector General, Department of the Air Force
Office of the Deputy Assistant Secretary for Environment, Safety, and Occupational
Health*

Congressional Committees

Senate Subcommittee on Defense, Committee on Appropriations
Senate Committee on Armed Services
Senate Committee on Homeland Security and Governmental Affairs
House Subcommittee on Defense, Committee on Appropriations
House Committee on Armed Services
House Committee on Oversight and Government Reform

* Recipients of the draft report

Appendix G. Acronyms Used in this Report

CPMS	Civilian Personnel Management Service
DMIPP	DoD Military Injury Prevention Priorities (Working Group)
ASD(HA)	Assistant Secretary of Defense for Health Affairs
USD(AT&L)	Under Secretary of Defense for Acquisition, Technology, and Logistics
USD(P&R)	Under Secretary of Defense for Personnel & Readiness